Table of Contents

Philosophy

When asked by the school psychologist what he felt was the hardest thing in school, a child replied, "The walls, I guess." If asked the same question, many teachers might respond that motivating our students to read is the hardest thing in school. Many of us have tried to combine creative writing with reading books and writing book reports in an attempt to motivate students to read. Somehow, this has not created the avid readers we all hoped for. As important as both independent reading skills and creative writing skills are, they do not always have to be tackled simultaneously.

The projects in this book will help you develop book reporting skills in your students. They provide an approach that concentrates on developing independent reading. They simplify book report writing and give the students a fresh and motivating new start each month. This book gives you, as a teacher, a program for book reports that will carry you through the entire year while it provides a large choice of bulletin board ideas for each month. The program provides an easy way for you to monitor students' book reports and to display and share them. This approach satisfies the objectives of book report writing by encouraging reading and by focusing more on the reading and less on the book report writing (thereby allowing the students more time to read). It also provides for feedback so you have some idea of what the students are reading and comprehending.

There may not be an approach to writing book reports that will make our students want to write more of them, but if we make book report writing more fun, maybe students will actually read more books. Isn't that what we really want?

How to Use This Book

Choose a Monthly Theme

This book provides themes related to the four seasons and to special days throughout the year. Select a different theme each month to captivate the students' interest and focus their attention. Several captions or slogans are suggested for each theme.

Create a Display Area

Designate a bulletin board or wall space that can be used for an ongoing book report display. Cover it with appropriate background paper, add the slogan, and put up suggested embellishments.

Involve Your Students

Discuss the theme of the month with your students. Encourage them to share experiences and knowledge related to the theme.

Explain the Theme Project

Give clear directions for the theme project. Let students brainstorm ways of personalizing their projects. Supply the suggested materials and provide time for the students to complete their projects. Attach the students' projects to the bulletin board with pushpins.

Set a Reading Goal

Set a reading goal for the month. You may wish to specify a number of books. Set the same goal for all the students or work with each student or group to establish more personalized goals.

THIS MONTH I WANT YOU TO READ ONE MORE BOOK THAN YOU DID LAST MONTH.

Reproduce the Book Report Form

Each student project has a corresponding book report form. Place an ample supply of forms where students can obtain them as needed. Be sure students understand how to complete the book report form. Set up a system to collect, check, and record the completed book report forms. Use the reproducible teacher and student record sheets on pages 62 and 63 to keep track of the students' reading.

Display the Book Report Forms

As a student completes a book report form, place it under the student's project. The project will serve as a cover for the displayed book report. When someone wants to read the book report, he simply lifts the cover and reads. Each form a student completes can be placed on top of the previous one. You may prefer to mount the students' book report forms on top of the project. If you choose this method, have students cut the project slightly larger than the book report form so that the project will not be completely covered.

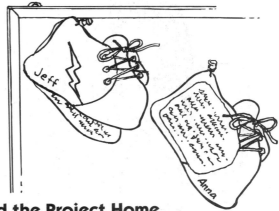

Send the Project Home

At the end of the month, remove the projects and book report forms from the bulletin board and staple them together. Each student will have an attractive packet of his book reports to take home and share with family members. This provides a perfect opportunity for children to talk to their parents about the books they've read.

FS-33002 Book Report Projects—Primary

Shortcuts and Other Good Ideas

The Bulletin Board Display

1. Enlargements—For some themes, you may wish to enlarge the student project picture to make a large picture for your bulletin board. To do this, make a transparency of the picture. Do this by using a copy machine or by tracing the picture on a transparency using an overhead marker. Then place the transparency on an overhead projector, tape a sheet of poster paper to the chalkboard, focus the machine to obtain the desired size image on the paper, and trace the image. Color the picture, cut it out, and mount it on the bulletin board.

2. Space—If your bulletin board space is limited, use whatever space is available. Display some of the reports on a small bulletin board with the caption and display the rest on windows, above and below the chalkboard, on the front of your desk, around the doors, and even in the hallway.

3. Display Box—Make a stand-up display by covering a large box (from an appliance store) with colorful paper. Print the caption on posterboard and hang it from the ceiling above the box. Display the reports on all sides of the box.

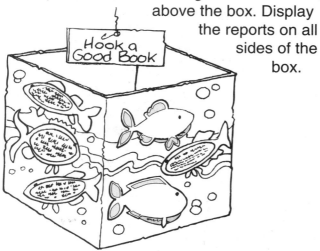

4. Lettering—For added interest, cut the letters for the caption from wallpaper samples, colorful magazine pictures, or fabric scraps.

The Student Project

1. Project Patterns—The outline around each book report form will serve as the pattern for the student project. A few projects require more than one pattern piece. Cut out of tagboard or lightweight cardboard a number of tracing patterns for students to use or show students how to place a sheet of construction paper behind the book report form and cut through both sheets at once. If you want students to write their book reports on shaped writing paper rather than on the book report form, have them trace the form on lined paper and cut it out.

2. Samples—You may be tempted to make a sample of the project to show the students, but your sample may stifle student creativity. It may be better to discuss a variety of materials and ideas with the students and then let them create their own designs. This will result in more variety in the finished projects and more fun for the students.

Organization Tips

Chart the Goal

Post a goal chart near your display area to remind students of their goal for the month. Try to spend a few minutes each week discussing the goal and the students' progress toward achieving it.

Check the Reading Level

For some students, you may find it necessary to preview their books to be sure the reading level is appropriate. Provide your students with whatever guidance they need to choose books that are suitable for them.

Pass the Good News

Encourage students to let their classmates know about the books they have really enjoyed. Provide book passes (page 57) for students to fill out and pass along to students they think would enjoy a particular book. This will help the students make good book selections and probably lead to more enjoyable reading.

Nonfiction Book Reports

If a student reads a nonfiction book, have him or her trace the book report form on lined paper and write answers to the following questions on it:

1. What is the title?
2. Who is the author?
3. What is the book about?
4. What are three facts you learned?

Inform the Parents

Reproduce the parent letter (page 64) and send it home when you are ready to begin this book report program. Each month thereafter, send home only the bottom part of the letter so that parents will know their child's goal for the month.

FS-33002 Book Report Projects—Primary

School Days

Captivating Captions

- Reading Gets You Off on the Right Foot
- Win the Race With Reading
- Off and Running With Books
- Stay on Track With Books

Bulletin Board Preparation

Choose one of the captions and mount it across the top of your bulletin board. Make a "Start" banner and place it on the far left of the board. Make a similar banner marked "Finish" to put at the far right. Cut several "hurdles" from construction paper and label them with the different types of stories. Include animal stories, number books, books of poetry, adventure, humor, sports, and other topics that your students might read. Position the hurdles between the Start and Finish lines. When completed, your bulletin board will resemble the track for a footrace. Mount the students' shoe projects (page 7) along the track.

School Days—Running Shoe Project

Have each student make a running shoe to enter in the "reading race." Mount the completed projects on your bulletin board display.

Materials

- patterns (pages 8 and 9)
- glue
- construction paper
- yarn or shoelace
- hole punch
- crayons, markers, fabric scraps

Directions for Students

1. Trace pattern pieces 1, 2, and 3 on construction paper. Cut pieces 1 and 3 from one color and 2 from a different color.

2. Punch or poke holes where indicated on the pattern pieces.

3. Glue the three pieces together as shown here, being careful not to glue the lacing holes.

4. Decorate your shoe using crayons, markers, or fabric scraps.

5. Lace your shoe with a piece of yarn or a shoelace.

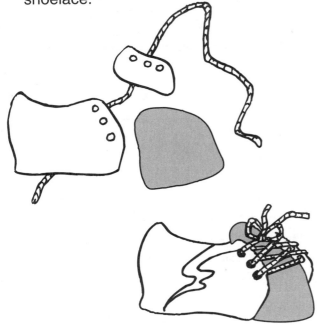

Bookmark

Reproduce the shoe bookmark (page 58) for each student. Give the students a bookmark when their running shoe project is ready to be mounted on the bulletin board.

Book Reports

Make copies of the shoe-shaped book report form (page 8) and place them where the students can take them as needed. Ask your students to complete one for each book they read. As they complete a form, have them cut out the shoe shape. Mount each student's book report forms under his or her running shoe.

Extensions

1. Cut out of construction paper a supply of simple footprint shapes. Each time a student completes a book, ask him or her to write the title and author on a footprint. Mount the footprints one after another on the wall. Challenge your students to circle the room with a footprint trail.

2. Have each student draw and cut out a favorite character who is running. Add these characters to the racetrack on your bulletin board. Take time to let students tell about the characters they have drawn.

FS-33002 Book Report Projects—Primary

School Days—Running Shoe Project

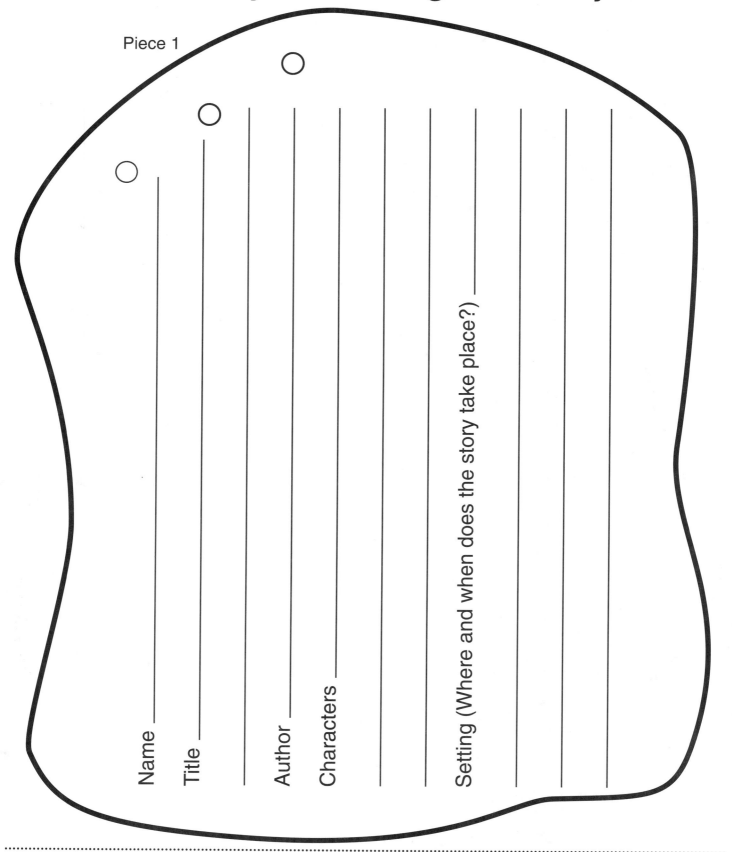

Piece 1

Name

Title

Author

Characters

Setting (Where and when does the story take place?)

Teacher: Use this page and page 9 as patterns for the running shoe project described on page 7. Use this page as a book report form.

© Frank Schaffer Publications, Inc.

8

a reproducible page

FS-33002 Book Report Projects—Primary

School Days—Running Shoe Project

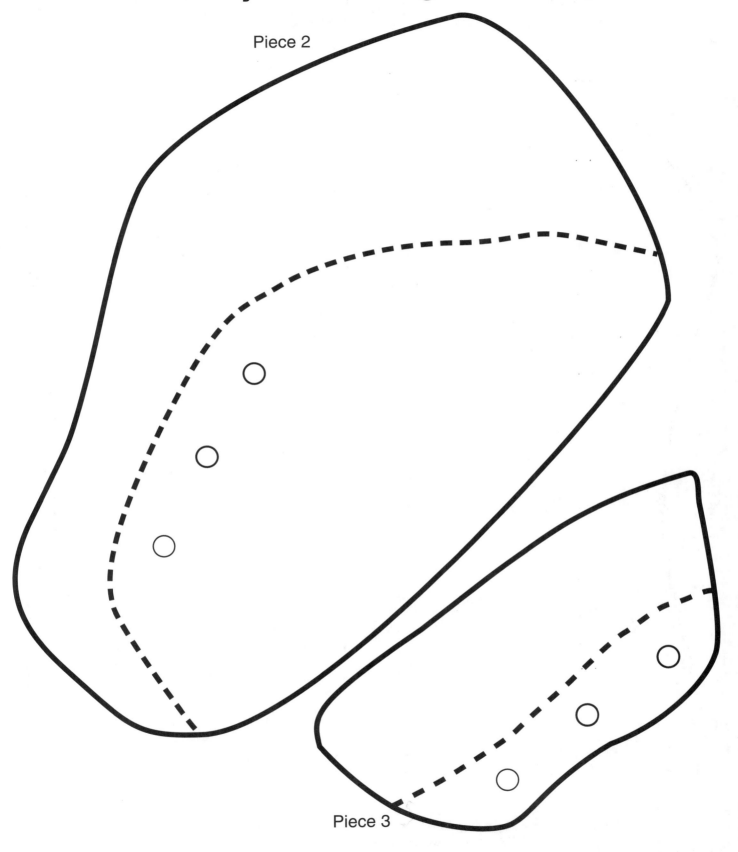

Piece 2

Piece 3

Teacher: Use this page and page 8 as patterns for the running shoe project described on page 7.

Fall

Captivating Captions

- A Bountiful Harvest of Books
- Books Are a Feast for Your Mind
- Give Thanks for Books
- Plenty to Be Thankful for in Books

A Bountiful Harvest of Books

Sam

Juanita

Greg

Bulletin Board Preparation

Have the students cut out a variety of fall fruits, vegetables, colored leaves, and nuts. Staple the cutouts around the edges of the bulletin board to create a colorful border. Cut a cornucopia from construction paper and mount it in the upper left corner of the board. Choose a caption and staple the letters across the top of the board as though they are spilling from the cornucopia. Mount the students' cornucopia projects (page 11) on the bulletin board as they complete them.

Fall—Cornucopia Project

Have each student make a cornucopia that shows things he or she is thankful for. Mount the completed projects on your bulletin board display.

Materials

pattern (page 12)

construction paper

glue

Directions for Students

1. Trace a cornucopia pattern on brown, yellow, or orange paper and cut it out.

2. On brightly colored paper, draw fruits, vegetables, and other things for which you are thankful (special people, your home, pets, clothes, favorite toys, favorite books). Glue the cutouts so they are tumbling from your cornucopia.

Bookmark

Reproduce the cornucopia bookmark (page 58) for each student. Place the bookmarks inside a straw cornucopia and invite students to take one when they select their first book.

Book Reports

Make copies of the cornucopia-shaped book report form (page 12) and place them where the students can take them as needed. Ask your students to complete one for each book they read. As they complete a form, have them cut out the cornucopia shape. Mount each student's book report forms under his or her cornucopia.

Extensions

1. Bring in a bushel basket or a similar basket. Have the students help you fill it with books about fall from their personal collections or from the library or media center.

2. Purchase a large pumpkin. Poke holes in the pumpkin with a dull pencil. Poke lollipop sticks into the holes. Allow students to "harvest" a lollipop as a treat when they meet their reading goal for the month. If you prefer not to use candy rewards, poke craft sticks or straws in the pumpkin and let students exchange them for a reward of your choice.

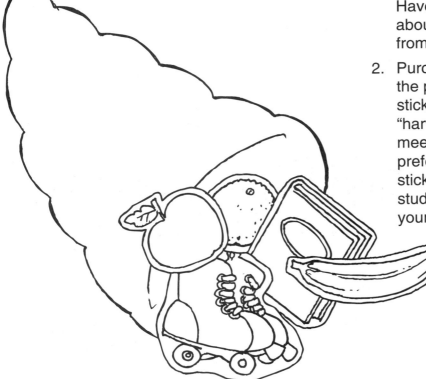

Fall–Cornucopia Projects

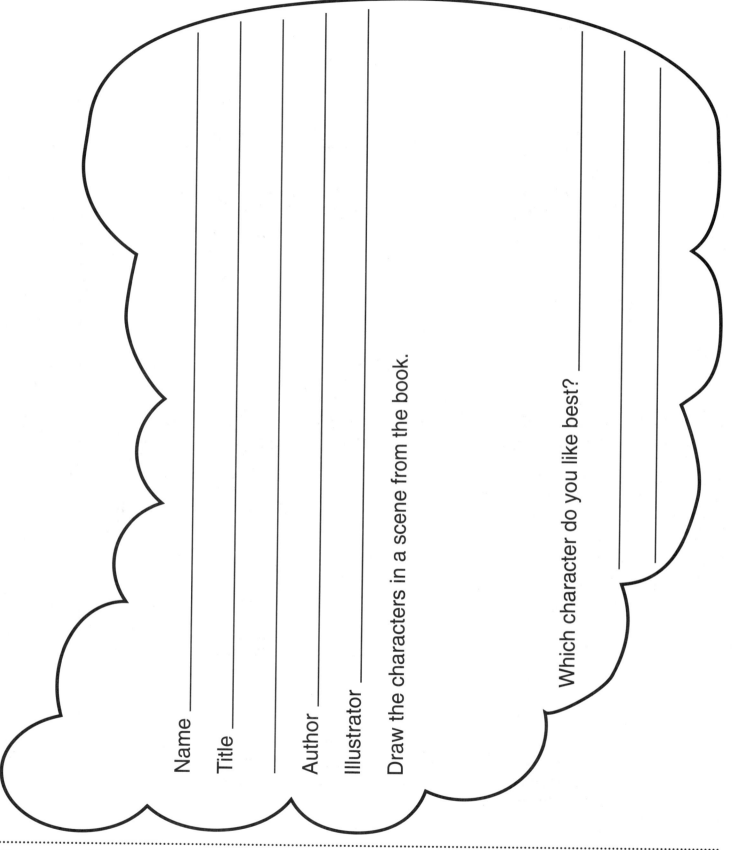

Name

Title

Author

Illustrator

Draw the characters in a scene from the book.

Which character do you like best?

Teacher: Use this page as the pattern for the cornucopia project described on page 11 and as a book report form.

FS-33002 Book Report Projects—Primary

Halloween—Spider Project

Captivating Captions

- Spin a Web of Good Books
- We're Crawling With Good Books
- Good Books Have Us Spinning
- Get Caught in the Reading Web

Bulletin Board Preparation

Cover the bulletin board with a dark color for a background. Use polyester fiberfill craft stuffing (available in craft shops and department stores) to make spider webs in the corners. Stretch the fiberfill stuffing and tack it to the bulletin board to resemble a wispy web. Add a caption across the top and mount the students' spider projects (page 14) on and around the spider webs.

Halloween—Spider Project

Have each student make a spider to attach to the bulletin board.

Materials

    pattern (page 15)

    construction paper

    glue

Directions for Students

1. Trace a spider body pattern on construction paper and cut it out. Cut points, scallops, or fringe around the edge to make your spider more interesting.

2. Cut out a paper head and glue it onto the body.

3. Cut eight one-half-inch strips for legs. Accordion-fold the legs or curl them around a pencil. Attach the legs to your spider.

Teacher: You may want to have students put their spiders on the bulletin board without legs. Put a supply of strips for legs in an envelope or coffee can and let the students add one leg to their spider for each book report form they complete.

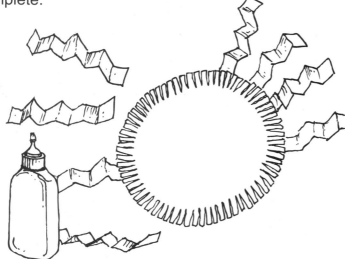

Bookmark

Reproduce the spider bookmark (page 58) for each student. Give one to each student as a motivator upon completion of his or her first book report form.

Book Reports

Reproduce the spider book report form (page 15) and make copies available to your students. Ask the students to complete one for each book they read. As they complete a form, have them cut out the round shape. Mount each student's book report forms under his or her spider.

Extensions

1. Have the students make Halloween masks of their favorite characters. Ask them each to carefully cut holes in a paper plate for the eyes, nose, and mouth. Encourage students to decorate their masks using construction paper and yarn to look like their character. Have them each write the title and the character's name on the back of the plate. Then have them glue a tongue depressor to the back of the plate to serve as a handle.

2. Supply your students with construction paper, yarn, and markers or paints and ask them to draw jack-o'-lanterns and decorate them to resemble a character from their book. (This activity will be even more fun if you have a supply of real pumpkins for students to decorate.)

Halloween—Spider Project

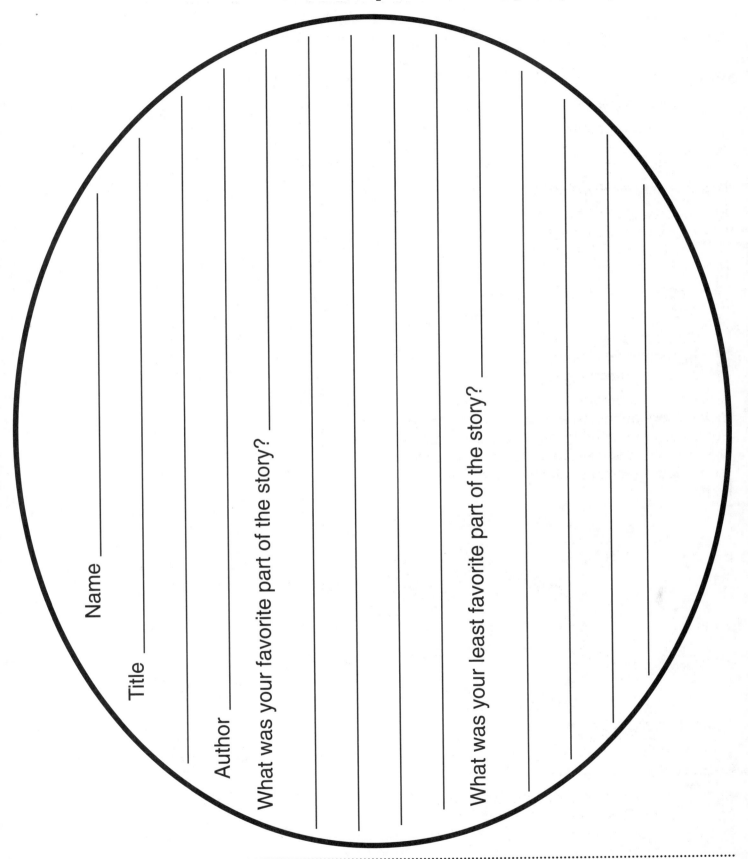

Name

Title

Author

What was your favorite part of the story?

What was your least favorite part of the story?

Teacher: Use this page as the pattern for the spider project described on page 14 and as a book report form.

FS-33002 Book Report Projects—Primary

Thanksgiving

Captivating Captions

- Your Library Is Stuffed With Good Books

- It's Time to Talk Turkey About Reading

- Gobble Up Good Books

- Turkey Trot Over to Your Library Today

Bulletin Board Preparations

Enlarge the turkey pictured above (see suggestions on page 4) in proportion to the feather book report form (page 18). Mount the large turkey in the center of your bulletin board. Choose a caption and display it on the turkey's body or across the top of the bulletin board.

Arrange the students' turkey feather projects (page 17) in two or three rows around the turkey's body.

FS-33002 Book Report Projects—Primary

Thanksgiving—Turkey Feather Project

Let each student create a colorful feather and add it to your giant turkey.

Material

   pattern (page 18)

   brightly colored construction paper

   crayons or markers

Directions for Students

1. Trace the feather pattern on construction paper and cut it out. Cut a feathery fringe around the edge of your feather.

2. Use crayons or markers to add feathery lines.

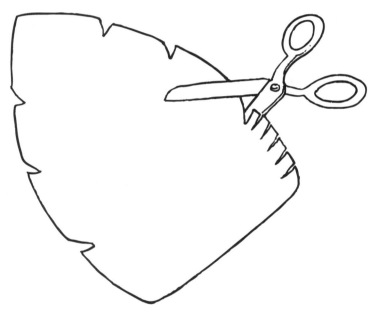

Bookmark

Reproduce the turkey bookmark (page 58) for each student. At the end of the month, give one to each student who has reached his or her monthly goal.

Book Reports

Make copies of the turkey feather book report form (page 18) and place them where the students can take them as needed. Ask your students to complete one for each book they read. As they complete a form, have them cut out the turkey feather shape. Mount the students' book report forms under their feathers on the bulletin board.

Extensions

1. Ask students to write sentences that tell what each character in a particular story might be thankful for.

2. Explain to your students that "turkey" is an expression for something that is a failure or a flop. Invite them to compile a list of books that are turkeys—books that they would not recommend. Insist that students give a good reason for any book they mention. Point out that their reason for disliking a book could be the reason someone else likes it. You may want to post a small turkey somewhere in the room and have students make feathers labeled with the "turkey" titles.

FS-33002 Book Report Projects—Primary

Thanksgiving—Turkey Feather Project

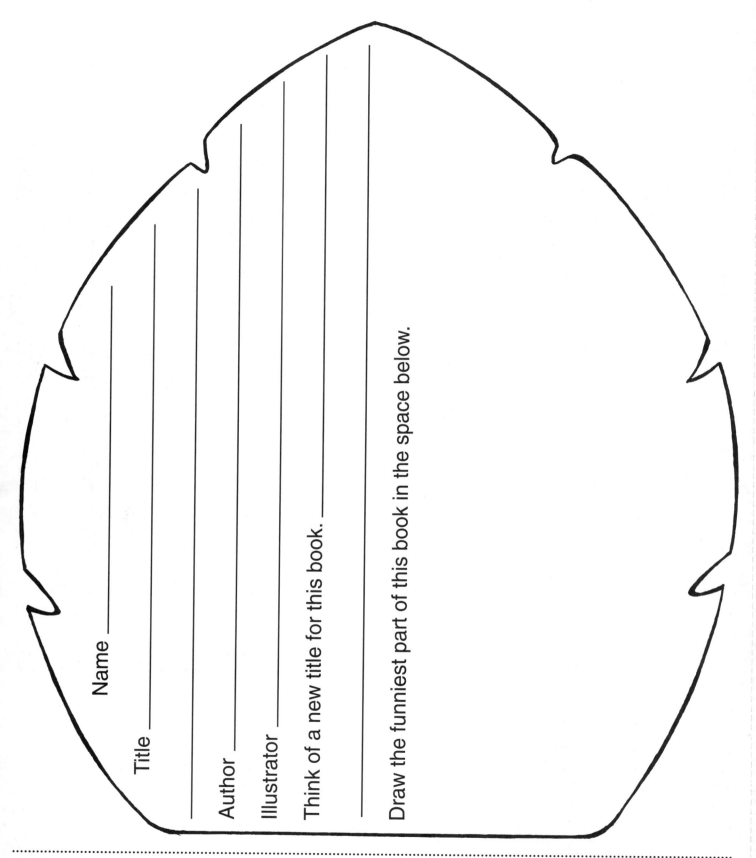

Name

Title

Author

Illustrator

Think of a new title for this book.

Draw the funniest part of this book in the space below.

Teacher: Use this page as the pattern for the turkey feather project described on page 17 and as a book report form.

FS-33002 Book Report Projects—Primary

Christmas

Captivating Captions

- Stocking Up on Good Books
- Books Are Filled With Goodies
- Holiday Treats
- "The Stockings Were Hung by the Chimney With Care"

Bulletin Board Preparation

Cut sheets of red, rust, or brown construction paper into thirds to make fireplace bricks. Arrange the bricks on the bulletin board in the shape of a fireplace. Leave small spaces between the bricks to resemble mortar. Make construction paper logs and flames and place them in your fireplace. Cut out several long strips of paper and piece them together across the top of the fireplace for the mantel. Arrange one of the captions above the mantel. Hang the students' stocking projects (page 20) on the fireplace.

Christmas—Stocking Project

Invite students to make and decorate book report stockings. Hang the completed projects on the fireplace bulletin board display.

Materials

- pattern (page 21)
- Christmas wrapping paper
- construction paper
- cotton balls
- pictures from magazines or old cards
- glue

Directions for Students

1. Trace a stocking pattern on Christmas wrapping paper or on construction paper.

2. Cut a white rectangle to use as the cuff of your stocking. Glue it to the top of your stocking.

3. Glue cotton balls onto the cuff to make it look furry.

4. Cut a heel and a toe of a contrasting color and glue them in place.

5. Draw a little picture of a favorite book. Cut out small pictures of treats such as candy, toys, and fruits. Glue your drawing and the pictures at the top of your stocking.

Bookmark

Reproduce the Christmas stocking bookmark (page 59) for each student. Place the bookmarks in a real stocking and hang the stocking near your fireplace. Let students take one after they have made their first book selection for the month.

Book Reports

Make copies of the stocking-shaped book report form (page 21) and put them near the fireplace in a gift box that has been wrapped so the cover can be removed. Ask the students to complete one form for each book they read. As they complete a report, have them cut out the stocking shape. Mount each student's book report forms under his or her decorated stocking on the bulletin board.

Extensions

1. Have students choose an item or picture of an item that would make an appropriate gift for one of the characters in their books. Ask them to gift-wrap the item and put the character's name and the book title on a gift tag. Then ask students to take turns opening the gifts and explaining why they chose the gift for their characters.

2. Organize students into five groups. Put the names of five authors your students are familiar with on slips of paper and put the slips in a box. Have a student from each group draw a name for his or her group. Ask each group to think of a suitable gift for its author and to tell the class its reasons for choosing the gift.

Christmas—Stocking Project

Name _____

Title _____

_____

Author _____

Characters _____

_____

_____

_____

Setting (Where did the story take place?) _____

_____

_____

Summary _____

_____

_____

_____

_____

Teacher: Use this page as the pattern for the Christmas stocking project described on page 20 and as a book report form.

FS-33002 Book Report Projects—Primary

New Year

Captivating Captions

- Books—Good Friends for a New Year!
- Ring in the Year With Good Books!
- Resolve to Read This Year!
- Start the New Year Right—Read!

Bulletin Board Preparations

Use butcher paper or large sheets of construction paper to make a large clock tower. Out of a contrasting color of construction paper, cut a large circle for the clock face. On the clock face, write the months of the year instead of the hours. Make two clock hands, attach them to the clock's face, and point them both toward January. Mount one of the captions above the clock tower and put the year below the clock face. To embellish your display, attach pieces of curled ribbon, streamers, and confetti. Display the students' New Year's hat projects (page 23) around the clock tower.

New Year—New Year's Hat Project

Have your students make colorful party hats for your bulletin board display! As a special treat, you may wish to purchase a special new book for the new year and share it with the students before placing it in your classroom library.

Materials

pattern (page 24)

white glue

glitter

shallow gift boxes

decorations such as ribbon scraps, rickrack, yarn, sequins

Directions for Students

1. Trace the hat pattern on brightly colored construction paper and cut it out.

2. Use white glue to write the year on the hat and to make wiggly lines or other designs.

3. Sprinkle the hat with glitter. Do this in a shallow box or on a sheet of newspaper so the glitter does not spill all over. Shake the hat over the box or the paper and save the glitter that falls off.

4. Add sequins, scraps of fabric, and curled ribbon to complete your hat.

Bookmark

Reproduce the New Year's bookmark (page 59) for each student. Tape or staple some curled ribbon to the top end of each one. Give one to each student as he or she completes a hat project and mounts it on the bulletin board display.

Book Reports

Make copies of the hat-shaped book report form (page 24) available to your students. Ask your students to complete one form for each book they read. As they complete a form, encourage them to cut out the hat shape. Mount each student's report forms under his or her hat on the bulletin board.

Extensions

1. Encourage your students to make some reading resolutions for the new year. Ask them each to list the titles of several books that they resolve to read. Encourage them to consult their friends for suggestions. Put the students' lists in one large manila envelope, seal it shut, and display it in a spot where students will notice it and be reminded of their resolutions. Later in the semester, open the envelope and let students see how many of the books they have read.

2. Start a class chart on which each student can write the name of a character from a reading selection and an appropriate New Year's resolution for that character. At the end of the month, plan a time when students can share their reasons for choosing the resolutions.

New Year—New Year's Hat Project

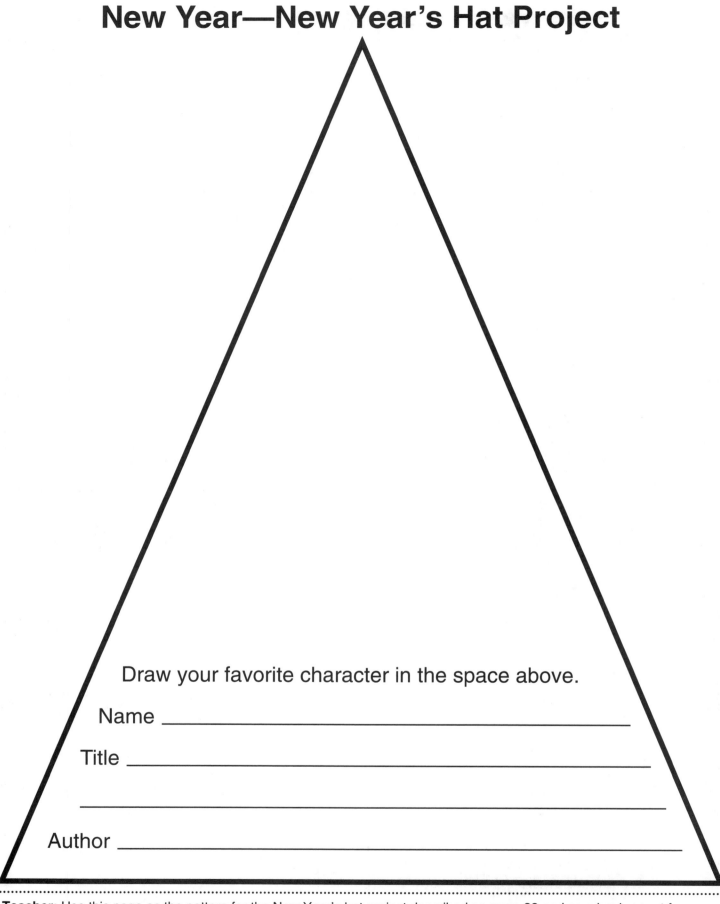

Draw your favorite character in the space above.

Name _____

Title _____

_____

Author _____

Teacher: Use this page as the pattern for the New Year's hat project described on page 23 and as a book report form.

FS-33002 Book Report Projects—Primary

Winter

Captivating Captions

- It's "Snow" Joke—Reading Is Fun!
- Books Take the Chill Out of Winter

- Warm Up With a Good Book!
- Here It Is in Black and White—Reading Is Fun!

Bulletin Board Preparation

Cut out of gray or light blue paper a large ice slab shaped like the one pictured above. Mount it across the top of your bulletin board. Cut out the letters for your caption and mount them as if they are floating on the ice slab. To create the effect of drifting snow, staple cotton balls or polyester fiberfill stuffing around the words and across the display area. You may prefer to cut drifts out of construction paper. Mount the students' penguin projects (page 26) below the caption.

Winter—Penguin Project

Have each student make a penguin for the iceberg scene on your bulletin board.

Materials

    patterns (pages 27 and 28)

    12" x 18" black construction paper

    9" x 12" white construction paper

    4½" x 5½" orange or yellow construction paper

Directions for Students

1. Fold a sheet of black paper in half the short way.

2. Place the body pattern on the fold and trace it. Cut out the body and unfold it.

3. Trace the chest pattern on white paper and the beak and feet on orange or yellow paper. Cut out the pieces.

4. Glue the pieces onto the penguin's body. Bend in the edges of the body to look like wings.

5. Use construction-paper scraps to add details such as eyes, hat, scarf, skis, and ice skates.

Book Reports

Make copies of the oval book report form (page 28) and place them near the bulletin board display. Ask your students to complete one for each book they read. As they complete a report, have them cut out the oval shape. Mount each student's book reports on his or her penguin's chest on the bulletin board.

Bookmark

Reproduce the penguin bookmark (page 59) for each student. Give a bookmark as a reward when a student finishes his or her first report for the penguin display.

Extensions

1. Provide small, medium, and large circles of white paper. Ask students to write a book title on a small circle, the name of the book's author on a medium circle, and an event from the book on the large circle. Combine all the circles. Then challenge students to find the circles that go together and arrange them to form snowmen.

2. Have students choose a book character and list activities the character might enjoy in winter. Have them explain their ideas.

Winter—Penguin Project

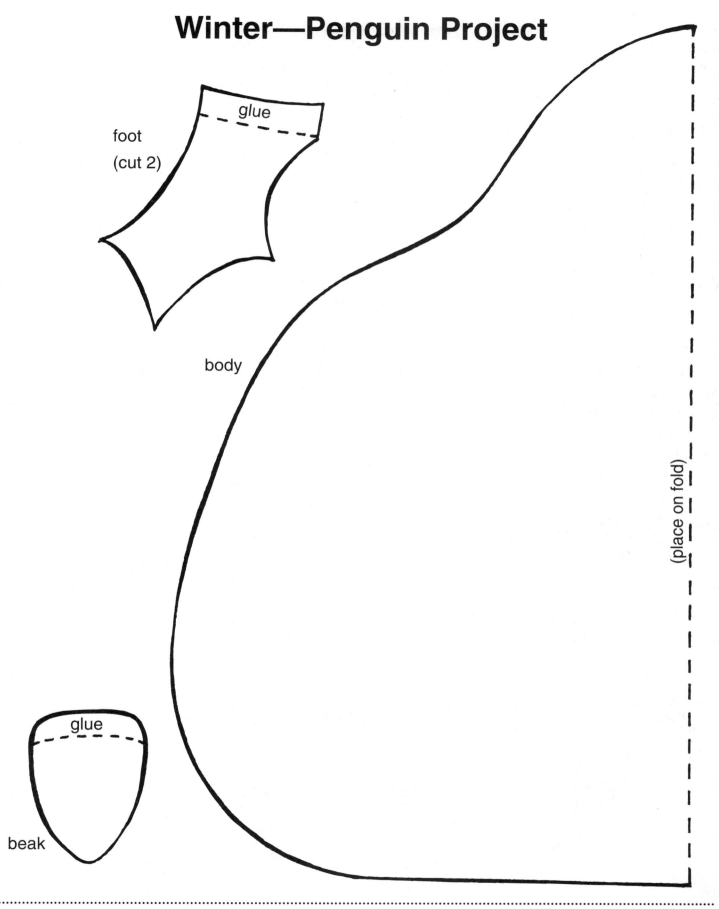

foot
(cut 2)

glue

body

(place on fold)

glue

beak

Teacher: Use this page and page 28 as patterns for the penguin project described on page 26.

© Frank Schaffer Publications, Inc.

27

a reproducible page

FS-33002 Book Report Projects—Primary

Winter—Penguin Project

Name _____

Title _____

_____

Author _____

Write about a character you would like for a friend.

_____

_____

_____

_____

_____

_____

_____

_____

_____

Teacher: Use this page and page 27 as patterns for the penguin project described on page 26 and use this page as a book report form.

FS-33002 Book Report Projects—Primary

Valentine's Day

Captivating Captions

- Reading—Put Your Heart Into It!
- I ♡ the Library

- Reading Is My Heart's Desire
- Get to the Heart of the Matter—Read!

Bulletin Board Preparation

Cover your bulletin board with pink or white background paper. Mount the caption of your choice across the top. Choose several "heart" phrases from the list below. Write each phrase on a strip of white paper, replacing the word heart with a red heart. Scatter the phrases across the bulletin board. Mount the students' heart projects (page 30) between the phrases.

The Heart of the Matter	My Heart's Desire	You've Got Heart
Put Your Heart Into It!	Heart of Gold	Be My Sweetheart!
The Queen of Hearts	Cross Your Heart	Have a Heart!
You Warm My Heart		

Valentine's Day—Heart Project

Invite students to create decorative hearts for your Valentine's Day book report display.

Materials

pattern (page 31)

9" x 12" construction paper in Valentine colors

glue

cellophane, tissue paper, or clear food wrap

Directions for Students

1. Trace the heart pattern on two sheets of construction paper. Cut out the hearts.

2. Cut interesting shapes out of the middle of one of the hearts.

3. Tape a piece of cellophane, tissue paper, or food wrap to the back of the heart with the cutouts.

4. Staple the hearts together.

Book Report

Make copies of the heart book report form (page 31) and put them where they are easily available to your students. Ask the students to complete one form for each book they read. As they complete a form, have them cut out the heart shape. Mount each student's reports on the bulletin board beneath his or her heart.

Bookmark

Reproduce the heart bookmark (page 59) for each student. Give one to each student as a reward for completing his or her monthly reading goal.

Extension

Make the familiar "I ♡." bumper stickers for several types of literature (I ♡ Mysteries, I ♡ Fiction, I ♡ Horse Stories). Put them up around the classroom. Supply your students with heart cutouts, and throughout the month, have them write the titles of books they enjoy on the hearts. Put each heart up near the appropriate "bumper sticker."

Valentine's Day—Heart Project

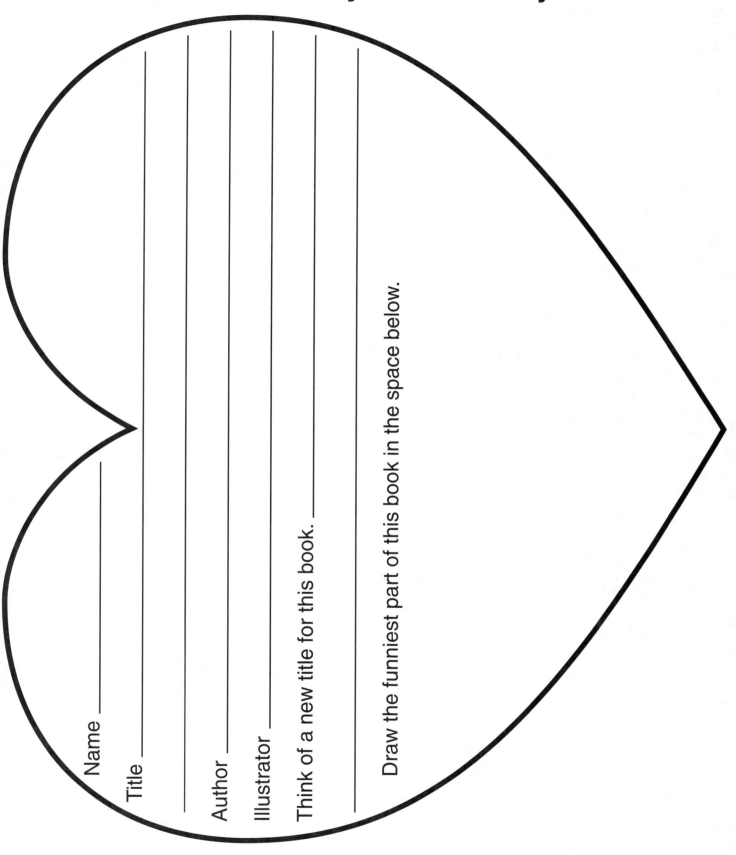

Name

Title

Author

Illustrator

Think of a new title for this book.

Draw the funniest part of this book in the space below.

Teacher: Use this page as the pattern for the heart project described on page 30 and as a book report form.

Presidents' Day

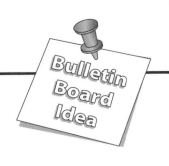

Captivating Captions

- Be a Leader! Be a Reader!

- Take the Lead—Read!

- Readers Finish at the Top

- Cast a Winning Vote for Reading!

Bulletin Board Preparation

Cover your bulletin board with a dark blue or red background. Mount the caption of your choice across the top. Have the students cut out small white stars and staple them around the edges of the bulletin board as a border.

Presidents' Day—Picture Frame Project

Let your students make picture frames in patriotic colors and mount them on your bulletin board to frame their book report forms.

Materials

9" x 12" red, white, and blue construction paper

Directions for Students

1. Draw a frame edge using scallops, points, or a fringe around all four sides of one sheet of paper. (See the diagram below.)

2. Poke a hole in the center of the paper and cut along the design you made. This will leave your frame in one piece.

3. Use a different color of construction paper for the back of your frame. Glue the frame to the background sheet.

Bookmark

Reproduce the presidents' bookmark (page 60) for each student. Distribute the bookmarks to the students at the beginning of the month. You may wish to motivate students by telling them that you will stamp the back or put a sticker on it for each book report they complete.

Book Reports

Make copies of the George Washington and Abraham Lincoln silhouette-shaped book report forms (pages 34 and 35) available to your students. Ask the students to complete a form for each book they read. As they complete a form, have them cut around the silhouette and mount the silhouette on their picture frame on the bulletin board.

Extensions

1. With your students, create a bibliography of books about presidents. Try to include books that are available in your library or media center. List the books and their authors on poster paper and display the poster in your classroom. Encourage students to choose at least one of these books as a book report choice during the month.

2. Have each student write a letter to one of the presidents. Have students recommend in their letters a book that the president might enjoy. You may want to have students exchange letters and write a response that the president might write.

Presidents' Day—George Washington

Name _____

Title _____

_____

Author _____

Illustrator _____

Think of a new title for this book. _____

_____

Draw the funniest part of this book in the space below.

Teacher: Use this page and page 35 as book report forms for the picture frame project described on page 33.

© Frank Schaffer Publications, Inc.

34

a reproducible page

FS-33002 Book Report Projects—Primary

Presidents' Day—Abraham Lincoln

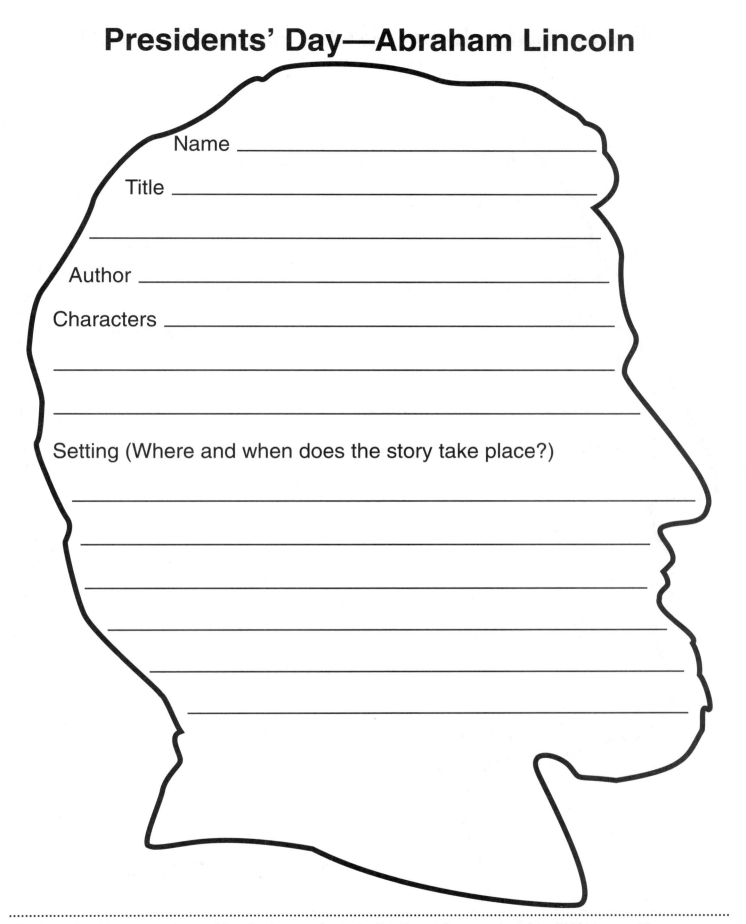

Name _____

Title _____

_____

Author _____

Characters _____

_____

_____

Setting (Where and when does the story take place?)

_____

_____

_____

_____

_____

Teacher: Use this page and page 34 as book report forms for the picture frame project described on page 33.

FS-33002 Book Report Projects—Primary

St. Patrick's Day

Captivating Captions

- Books—The Gold at the End of the Rainbow
- Get Lucky With Books
- Books Are Treasures
- Books Are As Good As Gold

Bulletin Board Preparation

Enlarge the leprechaun and his pot pictured above using the technique described on page 4. (If this is not convenient, draw or color a large rainbow across your bulletin board background.) Mount the leprechaun and the pot of gold in the center of your bulletin board. Cut small circles out of gold metallic paper or yellow construction paper.

Staple them in a heap on top of the pot to represent the leprechaun's gold. Cut the letters for your caption from several colors of paper and arrange them in the shape of a rainbow over the leprechaun. Mount the students' pot of gold projects (page 37) around the leprechaun.

St. Patrick's Day—Pot of Gold Project

Have each student create a pot and fill it with gold. Mount the pots on your bulletin board display.

Materials

- pattern (page 38)
- construction paper
- milk bottle cap or other round object
- glue

Directions for Students

1. Trace the pot of gold pattern on construction paper.

2. Trace several circles on yellow paper. Cut out the circles and the pot.

3. Glue the circles to the top of your pot, overlapping them slightly so they look like gold coins.

4. Draw or cut out shamrocks and decorate your pot of gold with them.

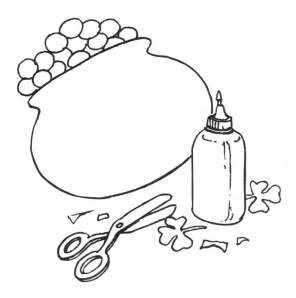

Bookmark

Reproduce the leprechaun bookmark (page 60) for each student. Store the bookmarks in a can that has been decorated to look like a pot of gold. Invite students to take a bookmark after they make their first book selection.

Book Reports

Make copies of the pot-of-gold-shaped book report form (page 38) and place them where students can take them as needed. Ask your students to complete a form for each book they read. As they complete a report, have them cut out the pot of gold . Mount each student's book report forms under his or her pot of gold on the bulletin board.

Extension

1. Cut out a shamrock shape for each student in your class. Make the shamrocks large enough for your students to write on. As each student completes a book, ask him or her to take a shamrock and write the book title on one of the leaflets, a character's name on another leaflet, and a wish the character might make if he or she caught a leprechaun on the third leaflet. Have students cut their shamrocks into three irregular puzzle pieces. Mix up all the shamrock pieces in a box. Then ask students to find the matching puzzle pieces and put each shamrock back together.

St. Patrick's Day—Pot of Gold Project

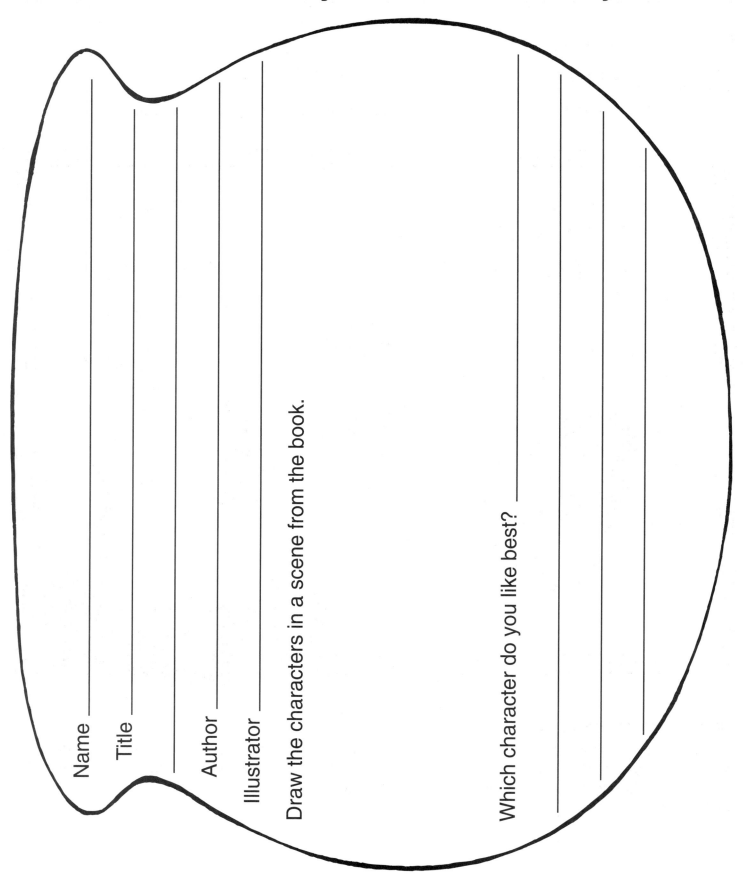

Name

Title

Author

Illustrator

Draw the characters in a scene from the book.

Which character do you like best?

38

a reproducible page

FS-33002 Book Report Projects—Primary

Easter

Captivating Captions

- We're Egg-ceptional Readers

- Eggs-ercise Your Brain—Read!

- Find Egg-citement in Books!

- Books Are Something to Cluck About

Find Egg-citement in Books!

Bulletin Board Preparation

Enlarge and color the hen and nest shown above according to the directions on page 4. Mount the enlargement in the center of your bulletin board.

Arrange a caption across the top of the board and display the students' egg projects (page 40) around the hen.

Easter—Egg Project

Materials

- pattern (page 41)
- light-colored construction paper
- crayon shavings
- newspapers
- waxed paper
- iron
- brass fastener

Directions for Students

1. Trace the egg pattern on construction paper and cut it out.

2. Place your cutout egg on several thicknesses of newspaper. Sprinkle crayon shavings on the egg.

3. Cover the egg with a sheet of waxed paper.

4. Carefully run the iron over the waxed paper until the shavings have melted. (Teacher note: You may want to do this yourself or have a parent volunteer help students.)

5. Remove the wax paper and cut your egg in half with a zigzag cut. Connect the two halves with a brass fastener.

Bookmark

Reproduce the egg bookmark (page 60) for each student. Put the bookmarks in an egg carton and allow students to take one as they complete their eggs for the display.

Book Reports

Make copies of the egg-shaped book report form (page 41). Place them in an Easter basket near your bulletin board. Ask your students to complete a form for each book they read. As they complete a report form, have them cut out the egg shape. Mount each student's reports behind his or her egg on the bulletin board.

Extensions

1. Fill an Easter basket with plastic eggs containing book suggestions. Invite interested students to choose an egg and read the suggested book for their next report.

2. Encourage students to create lists of "egg" words like those used in the suggested captions (page 39). Challenge students to use the words to create reading posters.

Easter—Egg Project

Draw a picture about your favorite part of the book.

Name _____

Title _____

_____

Author _____

Characters _____

_____

Teacher: Use this page as the pattern for the egg project described on page 40 and as a book report form.

© Frank Schaffer Publications, Inc.

41

a reproducible page

FS-33002 Book Report Projects—Primary

Spring

Captivating Captions

- Breezing Along With Books
- Books Take You Up, Up, and Away
- Soar With Books
- Spring Into Books!

Bulletin Board Preparation

Cover your bulletin board with a pale-blue background. Choose a caption and mount it across the top. Cut large, fluffy clouds from white paper or use polyester fiberfill craft stuffing. Add a sun and a few birds among the clouds. Make a border of small flowers to go across the bottom of the board.

(To make paper doll-style flowers, cut 9" x 12" sheets of paper in half lengthwise. Fold them in fourths. Then cut out flower shapes, as shown on page 43, through all thicknesses, being sure the flowers touch the folds on both sides.) Arrange the students' kite projects (page 43) in the remaining space.

Spring—Kite Project

Set the scene for spring with this project! Have each student make a kite for your breezy bulletin board display.

Materials

    pattern (page 44)

    brightly colored construction paper

    markers or chalks

    glue

    paper and fabric scraps

    yarn

Directions for Students

1. Trace the kite pattern on construction paper and cut it out.

2. Use markers or chalks, glue, and scrap materials to decorate your kite.

3. Attach a yarn tail and construction-paper bows on the tail.

Teacher Note: You may prefer to have your students put a bow on their kite tails as they complete each book report.

Book Reports

Make copies of the kite-shaped book report form (page 44) available to your students. Ask the students to complete a form for each book they read. As they complete a report form, have them cut out the kite shape. Mount each student's book report forms under his or her kite on the bulletin board.

Bookmark

Reproduce a kite bookmark (page 60) for each student. Give the bookmarks to students when they have completed their first book report for the spring bulletin board.

Extensions

1. Plan a kite day at the end of the month as a celebration for having achieved the reading goals for the month. Let students bring their own kites to school or provide one for class members to share.

2. Have groups of students create and illustrate stories about the travels of an escaped kite. Choose a reader from each group to share the group's story. Then post the stories where students can read them as an independent activity.

 FS-33002 Book Report Projects—Primary

Spring—Kite Project

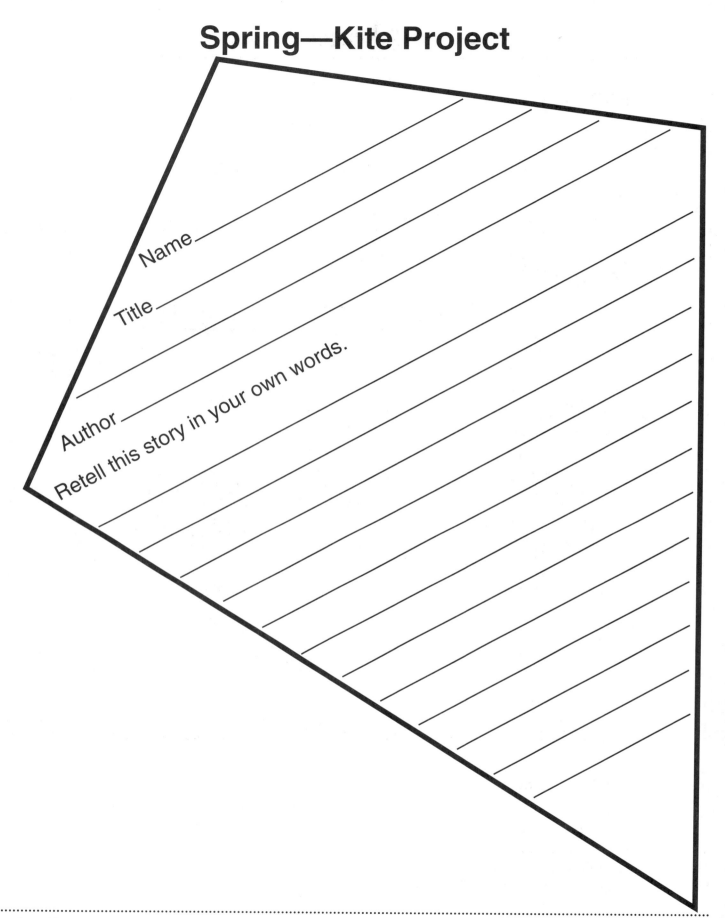

Name

Title

Author

Retell this story in your own words.

Teacher: Use this page as the pattern for the kite project (page 43) and as a book report form.

a reproducible page

FS-33002 Book Report Projects—Primary

Spring

Captivating Captions

- Don't Be Left Out in the Rain—Read!
- Books Shower You With New Ideas
- Without Books, You're All Wet
- Books for a Rainy Day

Bulletin Board Preparation

Cover the board with a pastel background color. Select a caption and post it near the top of the board. Cut a large blue puddle, several gray clouds, and a yellow lightning bolt and arrange them on the bulletin board. Mount the students' umbrella projects (page 46). Cut raindrops from blue construction paper and add them around the umbrellas.

Spring—Umbrella Project

Have each student make an umbrella for the rainy-day display on your bulletin board.

Materials

pattern (page 47)

construction paper

4" x 9" strips of brown paper

crayons, markers, or water-color paints

Directions for Students

1. Trace the umbrella pattern on a sheet of brightly colored paper and cut it out.

2. Decorate your umbrella using crayons, markers, or paints.

3. Cut an umbrella handle out of a brown strip. Attach the handle with glue or tape.

Book Reports

Make copies of the umbrella-shaped book report form (page 47) available to your students. Ask your students to complete one form for each book they read. As they complete a form, have them cut out the umbrella shape and attach a handle. Mount each student's report forms under his or her umbrella on the bulletin board.

Bookmark

Reproduce the umbrella bookmark (page 61) for each student. Give the bookmarks to students as a reward for completing their monthly reading goals.

Extension

1. Challenge your students to "flood" the bulletin board with raindrops. As they complete book reports, have students write the titles of their books on the raindrops that are scattered on the bulletin board. Add more raindrops to the bulletin board if necessary.

2. For a change of pace on a rainy afternoon, let small groups of students huddle together to read a book. Then have each group prepare and present a brief, impromptu dramatization of its story.

Spring—Umbrella Project

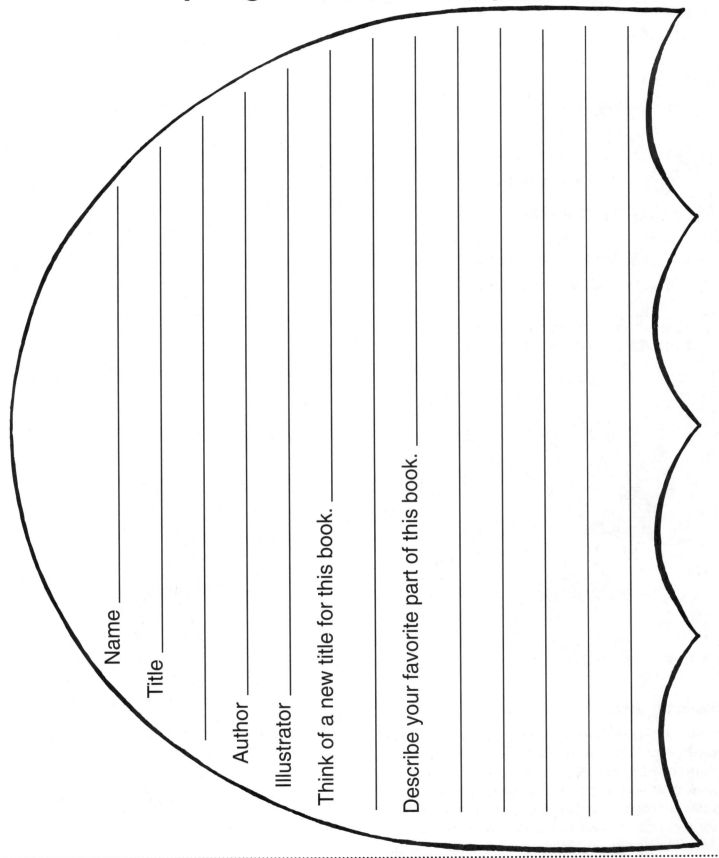

Name

Title

Author

Illustrator

Think of a new title for this book.

Describe your favorite part of this book.

Teacher: Use this page as the pattern for the umbrella project described on page 46 and as a book report form.

FS-33002 Book Report Projects—Primary

Spring

Captivating Captions

- Books Are Blooming Everywhere
- Plant a Garden of Good Books!
- Grow With Books!
- Find Seeds of Wisdom in Books!

Bulletin Board Preparation

Choose a caption and mount it on a green background. Follow the directions on page 4 to enlarge some of the "critters" shown above, or give your students drawing paper and let them design, color, and cut out a variety of garden visitors such as bugs, caterpillars, worms, birds, and snails. Use the critters as a border or place them randomly on the bulletin board. Mount the students' flower projects (page 49) on your bulletin board garden.

Spring—Flower Project

Encourage students to be really creative as they design exotic, imaginary flowers for your spring garden. You may wish to brainstorm a list of materials and techniques that they are familiar with.

Suggested Materials

> pattern (page 50)
>
> tissue paper or colorful magazine pictures
>
> construction paper and fabric scraps
>
> glue

Directions for Students

1. Trace the flower pattern on plain paper and cut it out.

2. Cut small squares of tissue paper or colorful magazine pictures and twist them slightly. Glue them onto the flower until the surface is covered.

3. Use construction paper and fabric scraps to make petals, leaves, stem, and other flower parts.

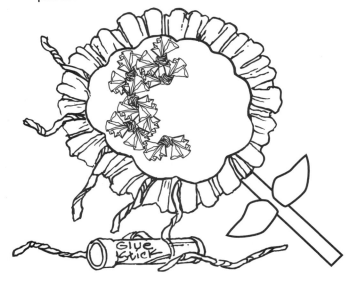

Bookmarks

Reproduce a flower bookmark (page 61) for each student. Distribute them to your class at the beginning of the month. As a motivator, put a sticker on the back or stamp it for each book report the student completes.

Book Reports

Make copies of the flower-shaped book report form (page 50) and place them where students can take them as needed. Ask your students to complete one for each book they read. As they complete a form, have them cut out the flower shape. Mount each student's book report forms under his or her flower on the bulletin board.

Extension

1. Give each student a small envelope. Ask each child to use the envelope as a seed packet for a flower that he "invents." The invented flower should relate to a book the student has read. Have each student draw his or her flower on the front of the packet and make up a name for it. On the back of the packet, have the child write the best time or place to plant the seeds, based on the setting of the story. Have the students fill their seed packets with paper seeds on which they have written the title, author, characters, and story events. Provide time for students to share their "book seeds" with one another.

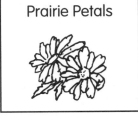

example for *Little House on the Prairie*

example for *Sylvester and the Magic Pebble*

Spring—Flower Project

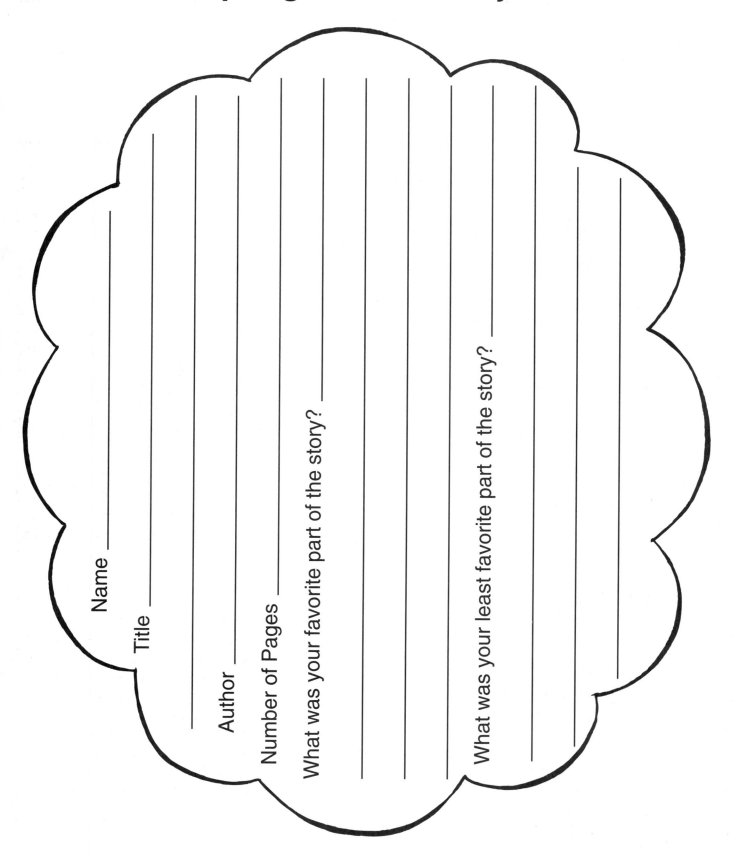

Name

Title

Author

Number of Pages

What was your favorite part of the story?

What was your least favorite part of the story?

Summer

Captivating Captions

- Fishing for Fun in Books
- Hook a Good Book This Summer
- Be a Bookworm This Summer!
- Get Hooked on Books!

Hook a Good Book This Summer

Bulletin Board Preparations

Cover the bulletin board with pale blue paper. Follow the directions on page 4 to enlarge the picture of the fishing bear shown above. Mount it in the upper left-hand corner of your bulletin board. You may prefer to draw a large stick-figure person right on your background paper. Cut four-inch strips of green construction paper and cut a grass-like fringe along one edge. Staple the strips beneath the fishing bear to resemble a grassy bank. Then cut four-inch strips of blue construction paper and cut scallops along one edge to resemble waves.

Staple these waves across the remainder of your board. Attach a section of bamboo pole or a wooden dowel to your board for a fishing pole or make a pole out of construction paper. Attach fishing line and a bobber to provide a three-dimensional look. Add a paper hook and a friendly worm on the hook. Arrange the letters for your caption along the fishing pole and fishline or across the bottom of the display. Mount the students' fish projects (page 52) in the water.

Summer—Fish Project

Have each student make a fish to swim in your fishing hole.

Materials

pattern (page 53)

12" x 18" construction paper

tissue paper, cellophane, or plastic wrap

glue

Directions for Students

1. Place the fish pattern in the center of a large sheet of construction paper. Trace the pattern.

2. Draw fins and a tail on your fish and cut out the fish.

3. Cut out the inside of the tail and each fin as shown below.

4. Glue tissue paper behind each opening to give a stained-glass effect.

Bookmark

Reproduce the worm bookmark (page 61) for each student. Put the bookmarks in an old tin can labeled *worms*, and place the can near the bulletin board. Allow students to take a bookmark after they have made their first reading selection for the month.

Book Reports

Make copies of the fish-shaped book report form (page 53) and put them in a clean minnow bucket or fishnet where students can take them when they need them. Ask your students to complete a book report form for each book they read. As they complete a form, have them cut out the fish shape. Mount each student's book report forms under his fish project on the bulletin board.

Extensions

1. Explain to your students that stories with exaggerations are sometimes called "fish tales." Have students recall books and stories they have read that use exaggeration. Help them understand that exaggeration is often used to add humor to a story.

2. Give each student a 24-inch length of yarn for a stringer. Have students tape stringers to their desks or along the chalk ledge. For each book that is read, have the reader write the title and author on a small paper fish, punch a hole in the fish, and attach it to his or her stringer.

Summer—Fish Project

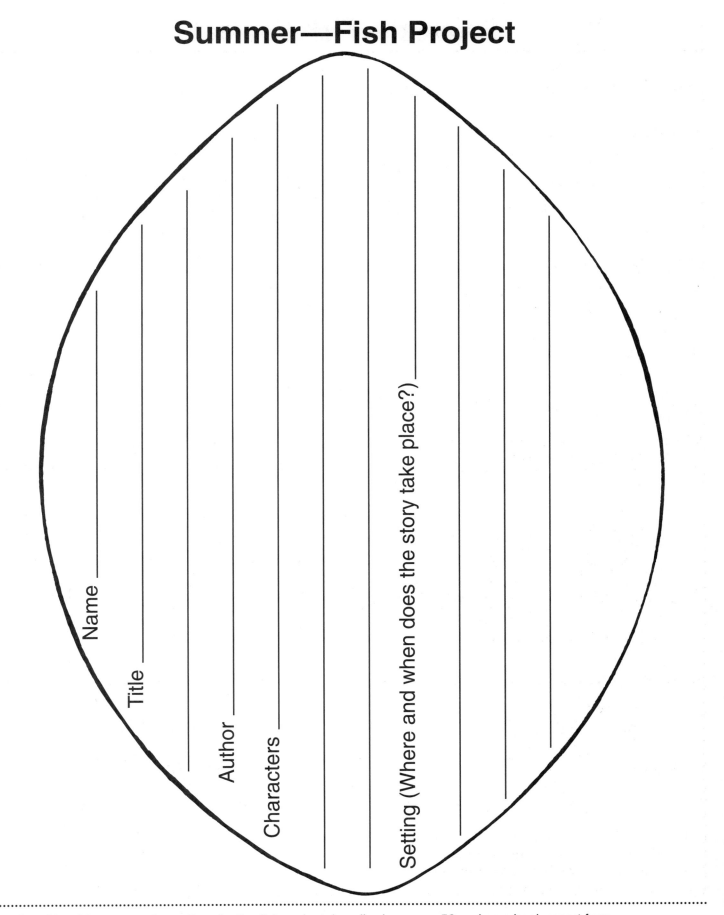

Name _____

Title _____

Author _____

Characters _____

Setting (Where and when does the story take place?) _____

Teacher: Use this page as the pattern for the fish project described on page 52 and as a book report form.

53

a reproducible page

FS-33002 Book Report Projects—Primary

Fourth of July

Captivating Captions

- Red, White, and Blue, and Good Books, Too!
- Uncle Sam Wants You to Read.
- Resolve to Read This Year!
- Wave Your Banners High for Books!

Bulletin Board Preparation

Cover your bulletin board with white paper. Cut a dark blue square and mount it in the upper left-hand corner. Cut seven stripes of red and space them on the bulletin board leaving six white stripes showing between them.

(To determine the width of the stripes, measure your bulletin board from top to bottom and divide by 13.) Cut out white letters for the caption you have chosen and arrange them on the blue field. Add the students' star projects to the display.

Fourth of July—Star Project

Promote patriotism and reading with this bulletin board display! Have each student make a star to put on the flag.

Materials

- pattern (page 56)
- white construction paper
- red, blue, and silver glitter
- glue
- shallow gift boxes

Directions for Students

1. Trace the star pattern on white paper and cut it out.

2. Use white glue to draw designs on your star.

3. Sprinkle the star with glitter. Do this in a shallow box or on a sheet of newspaper so the glitter does not spill all over. Shake the star over the box or the paper and save the glitter that falls off.

Bookmark

Reproduce the star bookmark (page 61) for each student. Allow students to take a bookmark when they complete their star project for the bulletin board.

Book Reports

Make copies of the star-shaped book report form found on page 56 available to your students. Ask your students to complete one for each book they read. When their reports are complete, encourage the students to cut out their star shapes. Mount the reports under the students' stars on the bulletin board.

Extensions

1. Make a supply of red and blue stars. Have students write on a star the title and author of each book they read. Add the stars to the bulletin board display. Set a class goal of adding at least 50 stars.

2. Give each student a 9" x 12" sheet of white drawing paper and a 5" x 4" piece of blue paper. Have him or her use white chalk to draw 50 stars on the blue paper and then glue the blue paper in the upper left corner of the white paper. Have students add seven red construction-paper stripes. Tell them to write the title and author of each book that they read on one of the white strips. (You could use this project instead of the star project on the bulletin board display.)

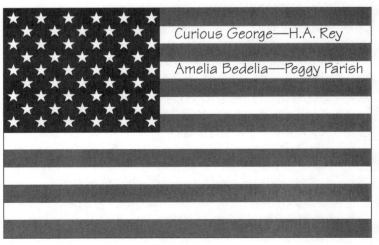

Fourth of July—Star Project

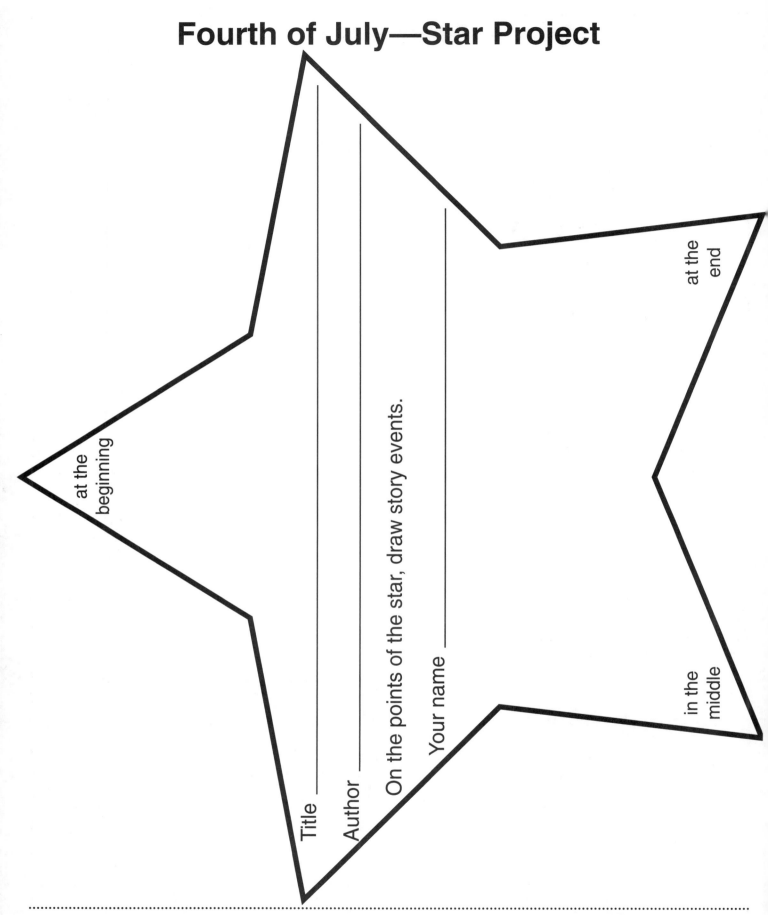

at the
beginning

at the
end

in the
middle

Title

Author

On the points of the star, draw story events.

Your name

Teacher: Use this page as the pattern for the star project described on page 55 and as a book report form.

FS-33002 Book Report Projects—Primary

a reproducible page

Book Pass

To _____

I think you would like this book!

Title _____

Author _____

It's about _____

_____

_____

_____

From _____

Book Pass

To _____

I think you would like this book!

Title _____

Author _____

It's about _____

_____

_____

_____

From _____

Teacher: Encourage students to fill out a book pass for each interesting book that they read and "pass it on" to a classmate who might enjoy the book.

Reading
Gets You Off
on the
Right Foot!

Read a
Harvest
of Books!

Spin a Web
of
Good Books!

Gobble Up
Great Books!

Teacher: Use these bookmarks with the activities on pages 7, 11, 14, and 17.

FS-33002 Book Report Projects—Primary

a reproducible page

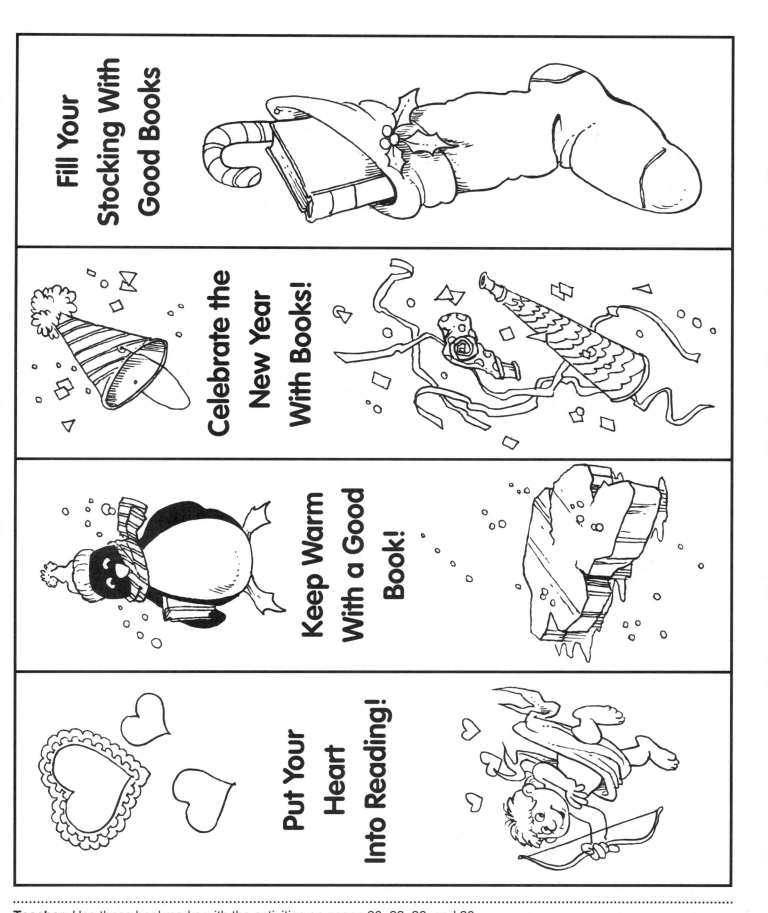

Fill Your
Stocking With
Good Books

Celebrate the
New Year
With Books!

Keep Warm
With a Good
Book!

Put Your
Heart
Into Reading!

Teacher: Use these bookmarks with the activities on pages 20, 23, 26, and 30.

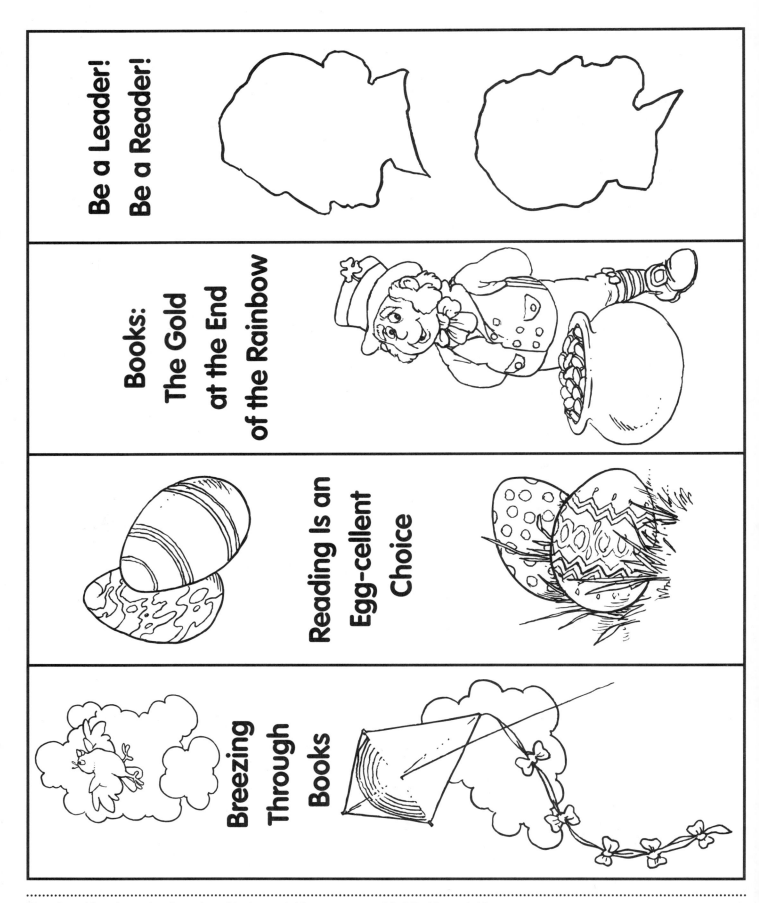

Be a Leader!
Be a Reader!

Books:
The Gold
at the End
of the Rainbow

Reading Is an
Egg-cellent
Choice

Breezing
Through
Books

Teacher: Use these bookmarks with the activities on pages 33, 37, 40, and 43.

FS-33002 Book Report Projects—Primary

a reproducible page

Don't Be Left Out in the Rain—READ!

Grow With Books!

Get Hooked on Books!

Red, White, and Blue, and Good Books, Too!

Teacher: Use these bookmarks with the activities on pages 46, 49, 52, and 55.

© Frank Schaffer Publications, Inc.

61

FS-33002 Book Report Projects—Primary

a reproducible page

Teacher's Record for _____

Student's Name																				

FS-33002 Book Report Projects—Primary

a reproducible page

Name _____

Reading Record

Title and Author	Date Completed
1.	
2.	
3.	
4.	
5.	
6.	
7.	
8.	
9.	
10.	
11.	
12.	
13.	
14.	
15.	

FS-33002 Book Report Projects—Primary

a reproducible page

Dear Parent,

Reading is relaxing and can provide your child with endless information. The ability to read well helps ensure success in school and throughout life. I hope to encourage and strengthen my students' independent reading skills with a book report program that motivates them to read throughout the school year. Students will set and work toward monthly reading goals, complete simple book report forms, and display their work on bulletin boards for classmates to read. At the end of each month, your child will bring home his or her book report packet.

Your child's name and reading goal for this month are written below. Please help your child find a quiet place and time to read. Be an active participant by helping with book selection, showing an interest in the books chosen, and even reading your own book while your child reads. Try to make his or her independent reading time as pleasurable as possible.

Thank you for your help and interest!

_____   _____

                  teacher   date

Student's Name _____

Reading Goal: _____ books

Teacher: Reproduce this letter and send it home when you begin your book report program. Throughout the year, you may wish to send home only the bottom section so parents will know their child's monthly goal.